ANAMNESIS

'I was intrigued and delighted by the originality and wit, the here-and-now "peculiar Eden" of the world she creates. Youthful, sexy, sharp, ferally female, funny'
LIZ LOCHHEAD

'Iona's poems hatch plucky, ponderous and pulsing; or do I mean louche, lithe and lasering? They're all of that, maybe more'
MICHAEL PEDERSEN

'Iona Lee is an exceptional poet, her work is articulate and perceptive and brimming with tenderness and authenticity. *Anamnesis* is compelling and beautiful, it is an exquisite poetry collection'
SALENA GODDEN

'The standout voice of her generation, Lee performs open-heart surgery on the English language'
DARREN McGARVEY

'Dazzling. Witty. Playful. Wild. Ingenious. It's easy to run out of adjectives when you're describing Iona Lee's astonishing first collection. "Is all fire the same fire?" she asks. Definitely not. These are poems of such energy and brilliance they will continue to burn in the memory long after the book is closed'

JOHN GLENDAY

'Iona's collection is a marvel. Full of beauty, wit, wisdom and surprise, delivered with the assurance of a poet who knows exactly what they are doing, it is to be treasured'

HANNAH LAVERY

'A door, a window, a rupture? The familiar openings and outpourings of *Anamnesis* are made strange and sacrosanct by Iona Lee, a skilful poet with a mastery of language. This startling debut is equal part stained glass as it is blood-stained'

DEAN ATTA

ANAMNESIS

Iona Lee

Polygon

First published in paperback in Great Britain in 2023 by
Polygon, an imprint of Birlinn Ltd.

Birlinn Ltd
West Newington House
10 Newington Road
Edinburgh EH9 1QS

9 8 7 6 5 4 3 2 1

www.polygonbooks.co.uk

Copyright © Iona Lee, 2023

The right of Iona Lee to be identified as the author
of this work has been asserted in accordance with the
Copyright, Designs and Patents Act 1988.

All rights reserved. No part of this publication may
be reproduced, stored, or transmitted in any form,
or by any means electronic, mechanical or photocopying,
recording or otherwise, without the express written
permission of the publisher.

ISBN 978 1 84697 632 2
EBOOK ISBN 978 1 78885 573 0

British Library Cataloguing-in-Publication Data
A catalogue record for this book is available
from the British Library.

The publisher gratefully acknowledges investment from
Creative Scotland towards the publication of this book.

Typeset in Verdigris MVB by The Foundry, Edinburgh
Printed and bound by CPI Group (UK) Ltd, Croydon, CR0 4YY

CONTENTS

SECTION I

Taking a Thought for a Walk	3
Lifting the Skirt	4
A Thousand Little Lives	6
The Simulation Game	7
Object Theatre	8
The Black Cat	9
Gallus	11
The Past Is Just a Tale We Tell	14
Suspend Your Disbelief	17
Beneath the Dead Man Mountain	18
We Two, Haloed, Hued	19
Notation	21
Lullaby For the Ferryman	22
Balancing	24
Girls	26
Bouncy Castles	29
In Lucie's Cabin	30
The Gardener	32
I Echo	34

SECTION II

The Big Dark	39
You Burn Me	41
Spell for Revelry	46
Play Thing	47
An Image of an Image of an Image	49
Abandon	51
Outpour	53
The Magic Word	54
Clink	55
Augmented Reality	57
Things That Are	59
View From a Train Window	61
On Receiving Unsolicited Poetry From Men That I Have Never Met	62
A One-Sided Conversation (i)	63
A One-Sided Conversation (ii)	65
Downfall	66
Anamnesis	68
Thin Place	70
Small World	75
Haruspex	77
Graveyards and Gardens	78
Nocturne	81
Love Poem	82
Morning After Elegy	84
Bowerbird	85
Acknowledgements	87

anamnesis [n.]
an-am-*nes*-is

– recollection, especially of a supposed previous existence
– insight, moments of unusual clarity
– an – un / amnesis – forgetting = 'unforgetting'

I

The first line thrown.
A tether tying me
to being.

TAKING A THOUGHT FOR A WALK

In art school I was told that Paul Klee described his studio
as being like a garden. At least – this is something that I recall.

When I was four, I watched the tattered bath mat reclining
like a gutted glove puppet on the cork floor and thought to myself
I will remember this – somehow, I still do.

I read somewhere that we walk through life backwards.

Words are not necessarily true just because they sound good. Nevertheless,
I believe in the poetry of that, like I believe in a painting's horizon.

I have watched my home receding through the slow rear-view mirror
of a car. I know how distance causes scenes to coalesce and flatten – yet
some instants glint, distinct as streetlamps, don't they?

So, for poetry's sake, let's say that it is true
that every morning, after breakfast, Klee would visit his studio
to see – in the subtle tilting of a new light – what each piece needed to grow.

Abstract art is meaningless as music.

For Klee, colour was mystical,
and over time his once depictive paintings disassembled themselves,
fragmenting, cadmium yellow and cobalt blue, into a peculiar Eden.

LIFTING THE SKIRT
For Sheela-na-gig

flash of flesh
sudden as 'is'
becomes 'was'
pink as the sun
through an ear or
russet, wrinkled as
the sand's wet fingers
shocking as a cold slap
of sea! ruder than
the pixiest of wishes
satin as deep kisses
with the taste of teeth
robust as my many names
read between my legs
this locket of splodges
                cave-dark
           calling you back
this numinous plumage
hewn in a weird workshop
this monster with cloven hoof
and hood, kept hidden, I am
the goddess of your belly laughs
                the good feel

sensory efflorescence, I am
the grotesque and happy
little instrument
untidy with desire
love-spell and soft briar
my only armour against
armies, against
harm.

A THOUSAND LITTLE LIVES

I was young and unaware in that most blissful way; Ballachulish / Ullapool / touring with my parents; Exeter / Pittenweem / a flock of half-remembered stops; town halls and little theatres. Iona / Islay / Mull. Precocious fabricator, I would tell my fellow children that mum and dad were tigers in a travelling show, or on the run. In truth, they were a thousand fleeting things. Kings / and matchmakers / and murdered. There was the cold, damp cottage in Pitlochry / the eerie flat in Hackney / where night fell close as a garnet curtain. And all the way up a ladder was a landing – heavy with fake flowers; the harvest of some factory in a land far, far away. I remember it like a garden, painted and unreal, where plastic petals bowed to the weight of glued-on dew drops. Frozen in tableau, the whole world holding its breath; so still and silver in the bewildering light of a dozen moons.

THE SIMULATION GAME
To be sung aloud

My speakers breathe
electric breeze
I plug into
the wind
the whizz unzips
the world wide open
and I wake you
from a dead
and dreamless sleep.

Raw little pixel, soul
of liquid crystal
I am the giant
face of god
tapping on your
fishbowl.
I gift you cherry trees
and honeybees.
Here's fireflies
to vibrate
on the limits
of your map.

OBJECT THEATRE

This is where they send sad kids
to try and talk them out of it.

Today I feel happy.
Today I feel sad.

This is the vocabulary.

You curate plastic dinosaurs
and Playmobil men
into the shape of your family
your friends.

Today I feel happy.
Today I feel sad.

This stegosaurus is my dad.

You write a letter to yourself
and never send it.
You are instructed
to draw your feelings as a tree.

You spend a lifetime contemplating
deciduous or evergreen.

THE BLACK CAT
For Lily, who lived on the isle of Iona

I am
the cat
who sits by herself
in the designated smoking area.

All you lot look alike to me.

See,
we were
worshipped
as gods once;
and I have not forgotten.

I am plant-like, purring.

Warm
in the
greenhouse
with the gardener.

Cabbage-shaped. Awake in a dream state.

I am
a thousand
year stare
on the dirt track at dusk.

Quite camouflaged by midnight.

Flying
saucers
of milk
mirroring the moon.

I am
roadkill
mangey
perhaps a little mad.

Bad omen. Black cat

with
the
upside down
horseshoe spine.

I have
seen the
other side
of nine lives.

GALLUS

I.

Jodi at dancing had a bit of an identity problem.
She would arrive. Every lesson, another story.

She was a princess in Africa.
She was modelling for Chanel,

draped along the backseat of a limousine,
wetting the end of a cigarette.

I had my doubts,
but if you ever caught her in a lie,

she'd laugh and shrug
with this grand carelessness

and slip the trap.
You've got to respect that.

II.

My flatmate's grandad kept dying.

He died at least three times,
always just after we had asked her to move out,

on account of the stealing.
Boy, could that girl construct an outfit from my stuff.

It was around then that Glo and I
met a photographer from Argentina.

We found her in the smoking area of this pop-up bar.
She told us she had tumours in her leg,

Three weeks to live.
I didn't even flinch.

We walked her home,
posing for her camera,

our high-heeled shadows
stumbling on ahead.

It was the wee small hours of the morning.
At the bottom of the hill, we all lay down in the road.

III.

Once, swinging on the swings in Neilson park,
feeling exquisitely feminine in my new beret,

I told a mother with a buggy
that I was from Paris.

Comment ça va? she asked –
which I hadn't seen coming.

Sure, I still lie sometimes, why shouldn't I?
Self is a collaborative construct.

If you ask me if I've seen *The Godfather*,
I'm hardly going to say no.

THE PAST IS JUST A TALE WE TELL

He wrote on typewriters
before typewriters
were vintage
(and the preserve of wankers).

His life was awash
with air-headed whores
who bored him,
and nineteen-fifties hospitals,
and red wine;
and you can tell
because he always made sure
to mention it...

I think it might have been easier
to be sincere
back then, before
everything had to be enjoyed
ironically.

Is it facile
to glamorise the past?
The starving garrett.
The dying beautifully
of consumption.

We shall never wander
through gardens, dripping

with ripe metaphors
sighing
We must make war with France.

Life is real.
We are people,
not projects.

But I am in the business
of romanticising.

When I look at the dark,
and the dark doesn't look back
and I feel overwhelmed
by the absolute insignificance
of everything...
my pen
pokes holes in the sky
so that I can breathe.

I, too,
want to make a masterpiece
of experience –

and despite the fact
that a nineteen-fifties hospital
was just a hospital
in the nineteen-fifties,

and that most great love affairs
dribble amiably
towards their inevitable conclusion,

you should never let the truth
get in the way
of a better kind of deeper
and more devastating...

SUSPEND YOUR DISBELIEF

For a moment –
The moon is made of cardboard.
Your father is a jacket and a hat
hanging from a hook.
The mimed meal has been completed
and everyone is full.

BENEATH THE DEAD MAN MOUNTAIN

      we eat and are eaten all over.
Half-rotten walnuts. Jewelled meats. Porcini
drowning in oil. An aubergine we all agree
looks a bit like a Moomin. Each fig is a wasp sarcophagus.
They fall in fat jammy droplets. I split one open, vigilant
for its sting. On the hot terracotta tiles, the little dog
licks herself with a deep reverence. In love from the waist down.
They have a saying here for someone that is excellent at eating.
Buona forchetta, meaning: a good fork. That night, wrapped
in my sleeping bag cocoon, I am caterpillar soup. Wine-drunk;
my dreams held together by cobwebs. We wake up in a cloud.
All day it is heavy, as an occupied hammock, swelling
with stormy anticipation. When the sky finally breaks
the raindrops fall as big as demijohns and we piggies go to market
where men sell umbrellas in the deluge and the flower stall's debris
is mashed into a perfumed pulp. We hide in the cool bottega.
I scribble some gibberish, while, beneath the table: the silent scandal
of his hand upon my thigh. When we cheers, our wine goblets
sound out like church bells. *Get it up ye!* we all say,
as the lightning takes a snapshot. Then the downpour
eats itself up and the grass is once again full of clicking.
I piss in the shade of an oak tree. I snooze in a hammock.
Beside me, a pregnant cat pads, clumsily, through the lavender.

WE TWO, HALOED, HUED

a rosy kind of golden,
filled-up to the grin
with newborn love.
And there's a lull
in all this sex and kissing.

We are insatiable.
Walking stoned to Tesco
to buy yet more red wine,
I am telling a story
that my mother told me

that her mother told her
and that her mother told her
about when her mother
took her aside on her
wedding night and whispered:

'Now that you are married, dear,
your husband is going to
gore you with his horn.
It is terribly unpleasant,
but you must get used to it.'

And then we walk
in silence, thinking,
a heaviness clinking between us,
all the way home and back
into our tangled bed,

where, supine; pelvis tipped;
hand on my belly; his wined lips
at the altar, worshipping;
his sheets begin to bloom
with poppies.

No wound. No
weapon. Not suffering
for no one, and no need here
to be silent or ashamed.
Safe, in love,

and we are laughing:
him with his mouth full, and I
for all the women – untongued
and tethered – whose blood I shed
in this wet, hot happiness.

NOTATION

When I wake, I keep my eyes closed, to keep the dream in.
A forest full of butterflies. Eyes opening. Butterflies, everywhere.

What woke me? The occasion of thought. Then a bus pulling up
outside – suspension in the key of A – sustained. A semibreve. A bow

on strings. I take a pen and make a note of it. I'd half expected
the outsobbing of a song. An overture, opening the day. Imagined

everybody singing; mouths opening, like morning birds.
O mouth, the first musical instrument. I write, try

to pin something down. Each letter is a note in language's songbook
and this morning's gathered notes into a tune that goes: butterfly, bus stop,

radio. Reader, the morning mind is gathering,
and morning is an orchestra tuning to the A.

What subtle and confusing music – these openings
in time's enclosure. Tuning

between the channels on a radio. The notes between
the keys. Thoughts as soft as butterflies.

LULLABY FOR THE FERRYMAN

~~Strung between sky   and   seabed~~

the little fishing boat, lilted,
anchored to something   invisible

The beneath   abyssal,

lulling its cradle hymn.

Can anybody sing?

a voice – a wasp
             unzipping the air.

The seals like it when we sing.

My mother is elected,
casts her line⸻

stilled rhythm
        held breath   and hush
                      now

                            hush . . .

                            and out of the blue everywhere
                              come their wet, round eyes.

BALANCING
After John Osborne

On a slow day in the pub
I asked Steve if that is when he felt
the most like a chef:

when he sharpened his knives,
taking big strokes, honing them
to a fine point. He said, *yes*,
but also when he chopped things
very fast.

I thought
and said that I felt the most like a waiter
when I balanced two plates on each arm.

I wonder if ball boys feel very much like ball boys
when they run fast and pick up a tennis ball.
Momentum. Efficiency.

I wonder if bankers look at themselves in the mirror
and say – *I am a banker* – as the reflection does up its tie.

Something happens
when you zip up that Sainsbury's fleece
or clip on your name tag.

Look at me
behind the counter
appearing in the role of Helpful Shop Assistant.

Today
I shall be sports centre lifeguard
with my knees and my whistle, I shall be glorious.

I shall sit atop a very high chair
and try to look like I know
exactly what I am doing.

GIRLS

You
dazzle cabinets
of dark and sparkling
        curiosity.

Arranged
in your careful nonchalance.

        Longing
to be unreliable
in an array of vintage negligees.

Playing it cool.

A pair
of black cherry lungs
        pendant
        in each pretty chest.

Thumbing well-loved lighters
        with the best of them,
        and relishing the burn.

Oh, how I do not envy you.

Those days,
they were heady
with drama.

On reflection –
        it was hell.

Falling
from one dream
        into another.

That first proper taste
of heartache.

The cold, hard shoulder
of the kitchen floor.

        But every day
                was another costume party.

Dancing down
the great banquet table,

gesturing wildly
with a leg of lamb.

Putting
your foot in it.

Life has made you sad
and filthy with strange power –
>   as brand new and ancient
>   as spring.

BOUNCY CASTLES

My ribcage is big.

Flat on my back
it blooms and deflates
like a bouncy castle.

Means you will live a long life
Mum used to say.

*All those birthday candles
with just one breath.*

I like those measurements –
a short ten-minute break
a wee pint

a long life.

IN LUCIE'S CABIN

I become
quiet

watching

the grasses
wave

the red cows
decorate a folded hill.

The evening
passes through
my wine glass.

Windmills,
such gentle giants,
spin summer

heat & breeze

to the buzzing,
copper-coloured thrum
of a honeybee

whose furious route
is briefly interrupted

by its own reflection.

THE GARDENER

Deep within a memory of mine
Mr Charity is introducing me to his garden.

Framed by the Rowan Cottage window
I can still see it – sloped, so.

He is walking me from bed to bed,
a doctor on his rounds,

bowing his head
to each brave, new shoot.

We arrive at the raspberry bush
and Mr Charity tells me

that a mysterious little ghost
has been stealing his raspberries.

My lips are stained blood red
and my eyes are blue.

I sometimes wonder
what has become of the garden

now that the gardener is gone.
Life will always fall into the absences.

A garden is not nature-shaped.
If left neglected, it will break its airy chains.

Perhaps the garden has grown interwoven,
wild; yet, when I tell it to you – it is tended to.

I ECHO

One ventures from home on the thread
of a tune – Marina Warner

You give me words.
Araucaria. Bactrian.
Crown the beech tree.
Get me on speaking terms
with curlew and kingfisher.
Teach me to listen
for secret harmonies.
Try to answer every question:
How come it never occurred
to the Romans to invent the bicycle?
And where does water come from?
When the earth was new.

I echo, becoming
a passionate scholar
of the well-told tale,
learning the stories of Pan,
the Green Man, Henry VIII
and his spousal disassembly.
From your great height,
you've seen it all!
In folktales, every father
is a poor woodcutter.
You are not a woodcutter
but you bring the forest to the door.

Then I must rehearse
the world without you.
In life, we all have
many parts to play.
The goody and the baddy.
You get the girl. The black spot.
Your comeuppance.
I belong to where I'm going,
but as you wave me off
I hear you calling after me
Be good, and if you can't be good
be clever . . .

II

The mote in an eye.
The tittle of an i.

THE BIG DARK

Once upon a time there was a wood,
a tangled map of paths. This is where the past lives,
deep within that labyrinth or enchanted loom
with all its tangled yarns.

Time turns differently
below the canopy. The forest roof,
        a cathedral's vaulted ceiling.
        Sing and she'll sing back to you.

We enter our little night-time
with reverence. It is a hallowed hall,
        this mouthful of twilight.

It strikes midnight
in the woodland's belly
        where each step is a prayer,
        each stone, a surprise.

Tapping my toes
to test the earth ahead of me.
Eyes growing fat with shadow.

The past was a dark place.
Winter would have been
        a giant sleeping beast;
        a wood without day dripping in;
        an uncracked egg.

It would have eaten me up.

In the absolute absence
of unnatural light, it is so much
easier to see

times turn: the trees taking back
what is rightfully theirs,

I saw it as we walked –
        the big dark ahead of us,
        and the big dark
        following behind.

YOU BURN ME

Time is the substance I am made of... it is a fire which consumes me, but I am the fire. – Jorge Luis Borges

I.

Legend has it that my maker wanted the world he had built for me burned before anyone could see it. Dying of a fever, Virgil asked that the *Aeneid* be destroyed upon his departure.

Thankfully for me – and for the world that was built therefrom – this request was carefully disregarded. Look deeper.

Legend within this legend says that I burned six books as a bargaining chip in business talks with a king. Six books of prophecies, translated into smoke, into formless thought. Books burn in a book-to-be-burned as Virgil burns up.

II.

All water is the same water and the same water that ever was.

Aeneas rode the Tyrrhenian Sea to the Cumaen shore to find me in my fabled cave. *A hundred doors a hundred entries grace; As many voices issue, and the sound of Sibyl's words as many times rebound.*

In one of many mouths, he lit a sacrificial pyre. Threw oil and incense. Is all fire the same fire? Oh, votive flame, illuminating all this time.

III.

I led him deeply down the cave's labyrinthine networks and out into the underworld, where this life is darkly mirrored, trembling in the Styx.

It is here, in that other place, that Virgil is rekindled in the tale of Dante and his inferno, arriving, not by cave, but by some phantasmagorical forest.

A thousand lacing corridors.

My cave of course is made from more solid material, and can be visited between the hours of nine a.m. to six p.m. – though it is closed on Tuesdays.

IV.

Myth and history are forever shedding their papery skins in strange loops. Plato's cave was allegorical, and his fire, metaphorical, representing the limits of our knowledge and reality.

One could cast language as that limit, what with its metaphor and magic.

I say it lights the way.

V.

Plato' tale – as Man's – sees an ascension from the cave dwelling. Out into Enlightenment. Whereas mine sees a descension. Dissension. A fall.

History is a story told by men. Even by me. I do not speak unless spoken through.

VI.

Undocumented, women's lives remain secret, hushed and hidden – in the margins. We go on in anonymous song; lullabies that ease the drop into oblivion.

It is perhaps no wonder then that our words were mistaken for furtive. That we were said to be possessed of *slippery tongues*. Fire speaks to fear. There were witch burnings, greedy licking flames consuming all that wisdom – limiting our knowledge. And book burnings. Pages taking to the sky, like so many birds.

VII.

There is a woman from the ancient world who speaks for herself: Sappho, though she survives primarily echoed in the mouths of men. She was born before the alphabet came to be.

What reality then did she dwell in?

What shape did her thoughts take?

Her work is scattered, largely lost. It comes to us in fragments, on pottery shards and papyrus – the memory materials which predates paper.

From what little is left we see that she suffers love like a medical condition. She has a fever. Poem thirty-eight reads, simply, 'You burn me'.

VIII.

Sappho was not burned. She may not have been real. One popular theory states that the bulk of her work was burned by Christians on 'moral' grounds – fearing that everlasting bonfire. What world might have been built upon her words had more survived?

We know that a complete set of her lyrics lived in the library of Alexandria, though there is no solid material evidence of the famous library's existence.

It is at least part-myth. A metaphor.

IX.

The library of Alexandria, if indeed it existed beyond anecdote, most likely mouldered, rather than smouldered. We can say that Sappho's works then were decomposed.

Papyrus, the memory material which realised the fiction of her lyrics, is vulnerable to rot. An example of creeping decline, rather than cataclysmic destruction.

One day, all of this will recede to the sea. All water is the same water and the same water that ever was and will be.

X.

After papyrus comes paper and printing. Dissemination of information and misinformation on a previously unimaginable scale, making the *Malleus Maleficarum* an early bestseller.

Fire and brimstone.

Then eventually comes that other world – the internet – but you can't burn digital files. Data centres store the material evidence of our digital traces, and simmer, not at fahrenheit 451, but at around 203.

It's too warm for people, but the machines do just fine.

XI.

Writing implies faith in a future – time being the substance of which it is made. The hope that, one day, we will all gather round and warm ourselves on our stories. Plug into the memory machine.

These days, the library is endless, and all the books are writing themselves.

But even data is vulnerable to rot.

XII.

Kindle the fire, and it will burn.

SPELL FOR REVELRY

Long live the smouldering perfume
       of your dressing-up box.

Long live the rosehips thrown
       at sleeping windowsills,
       the jewellery-eyed skies.

Long live the lunatic moon; the morning
       severed by half-sleep's languid shadows.

Bask in the happy, bee-deep voices
       that sing.

Long live the primrose way
       to the eternal bonfire.

PLAY THING

For the alien egg toys of the early 2000s, wherever they may be

An alien
enclosed in amniotic cosmic slop,
in psychedelic primal slime, part-primaeval,
you were molten. A million years all melted down
and selling millions.

We loved
your cold percussive shell of petrochemical,
your squidgable fingers. Foundling, you were foetal,
a poor defenceless cosmonaut. Not of this world, and yet –
your toxic star stuff was stitched in its beginning.

But more
than howking you, altricial,
from your Made in China egg,
experiencing your textures,
it was the lore we loved.

We swore
that you could multiply, by means of
ancient asexual magic, or fridge freezer. But
after months of birthing only gloopy bubbles
I declared you had deceased, and, ever ceremonious,

threw a funeral.
Interred you in a shoebox.
Eulogised you lost, and gone from us
forever.

Childhood
is single use. I've left so many friends behind. Yes,
potions master in the bath, purveyor of the tall tale, once
I was ring leader to a bedroom of blind eyes, bound
to my watch, with inner lives beholden to my quickening.

What a green fool I was.

Life is
a hotel, in which we never own a thing
and everyone I ever dared to call my own, continues –
in bargain buckets, junkyards, stuck to the underside
of upstairs or viscid in the deep beneath.

Relic for the mudlark.
Friend for the Tesco bag
jellyfish. Fossil –

you'll outlive us all.

AN IMAGE OF AN IMAGE OF AN IMAGE

The Belvedere in Vienna is home to The Kiss *by Gustav Klimt. Displayed alongside it is an exact copy, provided as a backdrop for visitors' selfies.*

They assume the position.
(You'll have seen a photograph before).
Two forms embracing on a flat plane.

Behind them,
in full gold leaf and jewel tone, the sensual
world in all its buzzing, folded, fizzing,
fruitful busyness and bloom.

A lush meadow, receding
towards a pixeled eternity.

He hooks his elbow into the crook of her neck,
makes a cradle for her head, her face
the picture of serenity. The everyday exhibition of love.

Paintings will become damaged over time
by repetitive flash photography. Like remembering:
each illumination – a kind of erosion.

This is the curator's best attempt
to protect the original from any alteration.

They take a few shots and move on quickly,
but later she will look back at the images
with an almost instant nostalgia.

Them in front of the Riesenrad.
Them in a café.
Them kissing in a photograph with a photograph of *The Kiss*.

ABANDON

Skulk along the bed
shoulder blades slicing like a tiger's.

Sly bodies flickering
in the mirror.

Oil slicked. Pink
tongue licked.

Dig a crescent moon
in petal flesh

with scissor
walking fingers,

pretty little
pleasure prisms.

The fizz of feeling
eyes on you; the friction.

Suspend me by a thread
from nothing.

Drop
and I will shatter

I will fractal
to a jigsaw

and almost all of it
sky.

OUTPOUR

Nautical dusk is
deep blue, ocean light spilled through
a stained glass window.

THE MAGIC WORD

little bottle, bright
as a mercury pearl
drop. ever so
elegantly necked
with bell bottom,
emptiness overlapping
a glass cabinet.
original liquid – long
since spilled, purpose
all poured out.
now said to house
a witch within
its silver shell.
I say that it's
no charm is trapped
inside that bottle
but merely an idea
(though both are
just as dangerous).
do you believe
in magic?
do you dare
to pop the cap,
let chaos flood
out from an
open mouth?

CLINK

After months of not kissing,
we didn't

                              A chance meeting
                    of eyes on the underground, lives
                 two lights at either end of a tunnel

Walking home from the pub
we lagged behind and talked
of nothing

                           A pair of feet fall in sync
                      with the beat of a song playing
                 on the opposite side of the universe

Until the silence of things not said
started ringing like a telephone
and the air between us flexed

                        A typewriter's striker misfires
                                takes a   breath

It was only a matter of time.
He took the hit. We got that close
before I pushed him off, thinking
of his girlfriend

                              A rocking chair is tipped too far
                         and teeters over the unsurvivable drop
                          before it's reconciliation with gravity

And that kiss that didn't happen
pinballed us off spinning
into separate lives

                            A snooker ball cannons and collides
                                    scatters the pack, like police
                                             at an illegal rave

If I could have my time over
I'd have done the bad thing.
Indulged in a little explosion.

AUGMENTED REALITY

Take some magic mushrooms.
Stoke the fire. Fall asleep
listening to a YouTube video
about the universe being
a hologram. Wake to a text
from a friend halfway up
a mountain in Nepal. Reply
with a waving emoji. Walk
through a landscape haunted
by clouds. Notice autumn.
The sweet smoke smell of
decay in the air. Have a sense
memory. Realise that I have
not been listening to the
podcast that I have been
listening to. Worry about
my attention span. On the bus
pretending to know how to
breathe. Google five reasons
to end your relationship.
Google can goldfish get
depressed? Pass a barbers
called 'Substance'. Another
new housing estate. Worry
that the future is behind us.
Delete my news app.
In the town centre there is

a handwritten advert for
Traditional Mole Control.
Call this number. Consider
calling this number. Take a
photograph instead. A dead
friend has left our WhatsApp
chat. Walk on through a day-
dream. Get lost. Look down.
Beneath my feet there is an
arrow. You Are Here.

THINGS THAT ARE

I leave our indoor ecosystem,
follow the map to where there is the promise
of trees and rushing water. I've missed them.

Only had a few square feet of world for weeks.
I want to see something far away: the sun
stride out in glittering ripples; hear
the polyphonic forest speak.

I whirlpool with people;
pause for every passerby,
a shiny little green beetle,
families out for today's
designated slice of the sky.

Everyone is saying

> . . . *when this is over.*
>
> > *I will, when this is over . . .*
> >
> > > *When will this be over? . . .*

The water is awake with fresh rain,
dark with waterlogged light. Sunbathing,
my eyes are left ajar. I watch a dandelion clock
as a breeze blows time away.
We have no map for tomorrow.
Things just are.

VIEW FROM A TRAIN WINDOW

a
murder
of
crows electricity lines
on

make
lyrical silhouettes
on
the
skies.

ON RECEIVING UNSOLICITED POETRY FROM MEN THAT I HAVE NEVER MET

Question for you – where does the internet end and a mind begin? The deep cavern that divides two hours / hearts / strangers – bridged. Eliminated, as if Keats himself had just burst in and flashed me. They glisten in my inbox. Expectant. Feathered. Waiting – for what, exactly? My adulation, I suppose. But I could be anyone, really, inanimate as I am. (Allow me to slip into something inconspicuous). One man wrote to tell me that his favourite word was 'devour', which made me feel . . . digestible. I wonder – had he ever told anyone that before? Had it been devouring him – or he it? Silently dining on devour's fricatives and long vowels. Wolfy. Toothsome, along the bladed edge of his tongue, as the two young sons who smile, apathetically, in his avatar, nibble at their quiet breakfast. Another said that he had paused the Tour de France just to send me the one about Van Gogh's missing ear. He had an English degree from a good university. What do I have? All the time in the world, and this bloody ear that doesn't belong to me.

A ONE-SIDED CONVERSATION (I)

'So . . . (about three pints in)
                    . . . do you know why aliens have never
contacted us?'
'Who's to say they haven't?
Perhaps their phone lines are wired to the other side. Perhaps . . .'
'No no no,
listen –
        the universe
is teeeeeming with life. Our little planet is an orb
strung on an *in*-com-pre-*hensible* celestial chandelier. But. The
rate at which information can travel is limited to the speed of
light,
        and the speed of light is
r e a l l y f u c k i n g s l o w . . .
Takes years
to get to the next star. Hundreds – if not thousands of years to
cross the galaxy!'

        'Imagine a conversation
        in which every exchange was separated by a hundred
        years . . .'

                '. . . When we first invented radio, we broadcast
to the universe. A bottle in a cosmic ocean.
Morse code. Sonar. Heartbeat.'
'But that period . . .

it's less than a hundred years.

        A hundred years is less than the length of one sentence between two people that exist on different sides of the galaxy. Less than a hundred years of transmission.

    That's a flash!'

        (Fingers click)

            'A lightbulb, flickering ... And that – is why all civilisations across the universe are, fundamentally,

        isolated.'

A ONE-SIDED CONVERSATION (II)

Outside, the city is relentless.

I exhale slowly; feel nicotine
deepening the moment, my breath
gently decaying, like a note.

The star's harmonics are a distant memory.
O, most ghostly bells. Address, unending,
with little hope of answer. Forever echoing.
O, smoke ring ... ring ... ring ...

DOWNFALL

I heard a crash
        looked up

to see smoke
bloom –

a white sheet
in a soft summer cloud

ghosts on a washing line

they danced
into my bedroom

blocked
my only exit.

I had been distracted
when I met my death:

a mushroom
slow as milk.

That moment –
an eternity, until,

as if by magic,
what had been smoke
turned to dust,

paused, as if mid-thought,

alighted
        whitening the room.

ANAMNESIS

He opened with a kiss. His tongue, a little hors d'oeuvre.
I nibbled it, before he left for the gym, suddenly overcome

with ennui. Is this what it has come to?
Exercising voluntarily.

Here we go, climbing hills,
and just to climb back down again.

Sometimes, I feel like a Babestation girl, but no one
is calling. Someone please tell me what they want me to do.

Sometimes, I feel like a video game character whose player
has left the room to make a cheese sandwich.

Sometimes, I wander aimlessly through Debenhams.

I want to feel so unbelievably alive. I want to dance
on a pirate ship, the black and pearl drop rain
bouncing like a giant's broken necklace

all across the deck. Not to answer the question
Where do you see yourself in five years? Because, honestly,

I chiefly see myself five years ago.

If only we could still play how we did
when we were kids.
>	Hold your hand up to your ear – the sea is calling!

I can be the mummy and you can be the daddy
and we can make a palace of this fallen tree.

We just need two bits of imagination to rub together.

THIN PLACE

I.

I go down to the beach
to notice things –
the homegrown happiness
the boats tethered on their painters
the whipped-white fringing of each wave.

      The lady
whose hat reminds me
that *life is good*.

It is nice to see such a positive affirmation
on a baseball cap.

It feels like the earth's very shore.

If you were that way inclined
I suppose you might say
that it feels a little closer to heaven.

      Hilariously so.
Yesterday, I saw actual dolphins
leaping in the bay.

And people always wish for dolphins
when nearing the edge.

The sea is postcard-blue
the sand cold with clean light
and benches bear the names
of those who have loved
this island before.

They come
in crowds off the ferry,
hooked to the view,
with the serene, ceremonious air
of holy people.

>	Where does one pilgrimage to
>	without a god to visit there?

I get the feeling that
everyone working in the hotel with me
is running from something. But
running from and running to
look very similar.

We need these small worlds.
To draw a circle
and step in.

11.

And it is small.

        I cycled
from one end of this earth
to the other in a lunchtime,
stopping only to admire
the rockpools
the respite
from the brimming ocean.

I had forgotten
how fun it is
to freewheel down a hill.

I had forgotten
what it is
to startle birds to flight.

        My world
keeps growing louder and larger
with every passing year.

My mind
is so full of voices.

Maybe I am shrinking.

Maybe I am just far away.
Growing further away
from the arrogance of youth.

III.

I've been thinking –
If you had a god to call your own
you would be in such close conversation
with the sky.

You would be so significant.
Your life would have a plot.
You would find yourself
in everything.

IV.

They call this island
        a 'Thin Place'. Say
that the skin between heaven and earth
is more translucent here.

And when I am serving soup to someone
I can look up, and literally see
the sky's conclusion.

The seam between
where the two dimensions meet.

I don't need faith
to find that sacred.

It does the *thing* to me too
where words fall, and all that remains
is the light.

SMALL WORLD

We lord over our land
from the bed we fell in love in.

Here, we are entire landscapes.

Sloped shoulders sweeping into bellies,
boobs, an expanse of thigh.
Toes out in the suburbs.

You pull smoke through a spliff
and it crackles like a radio.
What a warm, white sound.
Pins and needles to my ears.

My pet rats
run free around the room;
shimmying down a curtain,
venturing to the land of Side Table.

Busily being.

They always have so much to do,
and yet here we lie, like spilt custard.

I remember
one of them once made their way
under cover, and you were startled
by a tiny pair of hands
attempting to gather your left nipple.

That made me laugh,
the idea of those wee hands,
clasping.

HARUSPEX

Some strange lilac morning
we will take our bodies
and put them to grave.

Dew out our insides
upon the green. Quiet
as a book, they'll read

our cursive entrails, wet,
bleeding perils of wisdom
like pomegranate seeds.

GRAVEYARDS AND GARDENS

My city is as still as a watched clock.
The year repeats her days, reeled off
with as little passion as an actor
going over a familiar script.

I am decorating empty time, passing
my shadow between each streetlamp,
chasing a poem's tale around, visiting
the exhibits of my museum town.

In Edinburgh, you are never too far from a
body. They dug up three hundred the other
day. Left, lying there to reacquaint their naked
bones with a sun they hadn't seen in centuries.

Skeletons and supermarket queues. Time
is so elaborately piled-up on top of
itself. You could take a slice out of this
city and count her silver rings.

The past and I, we wind our
patterns round each other
like astrolabes. I am bumping
into ghosts on every walk.

Here we all are at eighteen, life
blood spilling from the quiet stone.

And here, down closes and up secret winding stairs,
the very site of that first kiss that didn't happen!

Or here, where I fell, attempting
to scale the garden wall. Someone
should put up a plaque to commemorate
that we were here and that we lived.

For the streets are now a graveyard
of old haunts that didn't make it. I
thought that I might try and dig us up, but
I've been finding it exhausting.

It is this worry I am walking
through the rain when, one
day, I spy a chink in the wall.
Scrambling over, I find myself

in Warriston cemetery. A secret
garden built from shards of epitaph.
It is last orders in Edina's deep
Underworld, where so many

dead are planted. Cenotaphs and
seraphim, merrily entangled in silent
celebration, conspire, sharing their
final words before succumbed to yellow

lichen or a drunken slump. I hope
that when my tombstone topples
it will fall face up. The whole world
holds its breath and my knees,

they kiss the green moss floor. I'm
digging up bone dust, the earth under my
nails, I'm dredging up green mulch and
searching for some skull to place a bulb in.

I'm hoping it will bloom.

NOCTURNE

We dwell not on earth but in language – Greg Garrard

The dreaming city
is blinking its evening rooms – a punctured
silhouette of jack o' lantern teeth.
        And deep beneath the skin of sleep
the flat is damp and beating.
We are wee beasties in the fat pulp
of a flower's pointed heart.
                Colour of the golden hour
                through an eyelid: egg yolk.
The night cracks open, honeycombs,
makes constellations from each lambent household.
Our souls hung up like ghosts to dry in arabesques.
        Sudden cobwebs.
        We are so many distant orbs.
But somewhere, down a dream-lit corridor,
I lift the veil, like a bead curtain, and whisper
your names.

LOVE POEM

One morning you awoke
   to find me in your dream. We kissed. The love poems of two strangers
            printed on facing pages.

In my stories we are always in bed.
Lift your head up from the pillow! I've a gift for your good ear.

It's a love poem, love. I'm licking
the back of a stamp. With the good tongue
strung in my head let me tell you this:
   There is nothing between us.

Me and my admittedly limited knowledge
of atoms and apples and gravity. (I've but a language cabinet
            for my curiosity).
I mean that there is *nothing* between us. Always.

Even after holding one another through all these years
you know that we have never truly touched?

It is thoughts like this that keep me lonely at night
as you set off, invisibly, down corridors that I can never wander.

I am in the archives of our shared memories.
Shut up like a tomb. The day interred.
I am turning our dark pages.

In my stories, I am always alone and talking to myself.
When I first learned of solipsism, I looked straight to camera.
       But here, love! Hear,
       the present – have my voice;
the door through which I leave myself and let you in.

MORNING AFTER ELEGY

This morning, I am mourning
my beloved: my beautiful blue velvet jacket
with the pantomime Prince Charming fit.
Charity shop treasure *(you'll never guess how much)*
and smooth as a midnight oil slick; star
of the moonstruck saloon. Forever lost
– not forgotten – but left, nonetheless,
to hem the silhouette around a stranger's shadow.
 All these holes in my pockets.
My soul still marches round in those red boots,
and we never did find Gloria's ring, slipped surreptitiously,
though we spent all morning snorkelling in the hot sun,
wishing for the ocean's *et voila!* What jewels she must wear
on her rippling fingers. All we have lost to the dark.

BOWERBIRD

August turned to embers
and everyone fell apart.

Tired bones wind chiming
autumn's rattle.

It was time to leave. To lay
my curiosities around me.

Apricot pip. Iridescent shell
and sea glass. Crab claw.

Button for a long, lost jacket.
A fortune, that reads

*Look for the dream
that keeps coming back*

in six different languages.
I don't know what that means,

but here is my wisdom –
Magic is the art of wishing well.

I collect.
I always have.

Pools of cold tea water.
Words. Lately, it's been mushroom names.

Listen – Shaggy Parasol.
Amethyst Deceiver. The Flirt.

My friends are all preserving
things in glass jars.

Kombucha and sauerkraut.
One day, we will be so healthy.

Moth-eaten butterfly wing.
Wire nest. Broken ring.

My threadbare treasures.
I don't know what I keep saving you for.

For something good, I hope.
Hopefully something good.

ACKNOWLEDGEMENTS

Thank you . . .

Dad, for the words; Mum, for the love; Daniel, for the years.

My dear cousins, for the camaraderie.

Salena Godden, for opening the door; Leyla Josephine and Colin Bramwell, for the encouragement.

Edward Crossan and Polygon, for the belief and support.

My tutors at DJCAD for the inspiration.

Jenni Fagan; John Glenday; Rachel Long; Hannah Lavery; Colin McGuire and Claire Askew, for the feedback and advice.

Eve; Ellie; Gloria; Mungo; and Molly, for the friendship and the fights.

Ruairidh, for the music; Lucie, for the cabin.

And thank you, to you, for reading.

The phrase 'ease the drop into oblivion' from 'You Burn Me', on page 43, is a quote from *No Go the Bogeyman* (Vintage, 2020) by Marina Warner; and 'creeping decline, rather than cataclysmic destruction', from 'You Burn Me', on page 44, is a reference, to *Burning the Books: A History of Knowledge Under Attack* (John Murray, 2020) by Richard Ovenden.